Native Fruit

Poetry and Fine Art Inspired by the Pawpaw

Native Fruit: Poetry and Fine Art Inspired by the Pawpaw
© 2024 Stephanie Kendrick

Editor: Stephanie Kendrick
Art Editor: Jessica Held
Cover Art: Chelsie Azbell
Cover Art Photographed by Michael Clemons-Stevens

ISBN: 9781962405065

Sheila-Na-Gig Editions
Russell, KY
Hayley Mitchell Haugen, Editor
www.sheilanagigblog.com

Inquiries: Stephanie Kendrick
Stephthepoet88@gmail.com
Athenspoetlaureate4@gmail.com

Native Fruit

Poetry and Fine Art Inspired by the Pawpaw

Edited by Stephanie Kendrick

Fine Art Editor: Jessica Held

Sheila-Na-Gig Editions

We build community by sharing.
Poems, art, food or seeds—
this book is dedicated to those who share.

CONTENTS

Chris Chmiel and Michelle Gorman
Preface   10
Attila Horvath
I Searched For Your Sweetness   13
Larry D. Thacker
Roadside Searching   14
A Communion   15
Cody Dikis
Pawpaw in Crayon   16
David B. Prather
Anthimeria Lover   17
Way Down Yonder   19
Jennifer Browne
Appalachian RE: Revision   20
Patricia Thrushart
Lewis & Clarke Survive on Pawpaw, 1806   21
Katarena Altier
Cycle of the Pawpaw   22
Jennifer Browne
Fourteen   23
Kari Gunter-Seymour
Pawpaws Are Ripe   24
Tom Barlow
Orphans   25
Heidi Joffe
Fenestrated   26
Anna Robinson
Pawpaw   28
Ross DiPenti
What I Saw Under the Pawpaw Tree   29
Lucia Carver Daniels
Pawpaw Ice Cream   31
Kristine Williams
Bombs for Pawpaws   32
January in Athens County   33
Wendy McVicker
Bon appétit!   34
Renee Williams
Mangoes in the Mist   35
Sherry Deskins Goodson
Juno Beach, Florida Pawpaw Bloom   37

Andrew Alexis Varvel
Roses are Red   38
Here in Bismarck, North Dakota   39
Jean Mikhail
There, You'll Find Them   40
Andy Milliken
Softening   43
Katherine Ziff
Good Morning   44
Here's my story of falling pawpaws   45
Grant Clauser
Planting Pawpaws   46
Rebekah Cotton
How to Make Pawpaw Pudding   47
Orinn Hohenstein
Pawpaw   49
Katherine Ziff
Pawpaw Trees in Winter   50
Chris Farrell
A Pawpaw Prayer   51
Amy Le Ann Richardson
Consider the Pawpaw   52
Ars Pawpaw   53
L.D. Nehls
Northside Neighbors   54
Jeri Kendrick
Pawpaws   55
Jennifer Michelle Mayer
Asimina   56
Pawpaw, Reversed   57
Stephanie Campsey
That Underappreciated Fruit   58
Rob Brannan
Pawpaw1   59
Barbara Marie Minney
A Brief History of the Pawpaw   60
Jessica Weyer-Bentley
The Sage Witness   61
Jason Baldinger
in an elk's eye   62
under a pawpaw   63
L.D. Nehls
Evolutionary Anachronisms of Burnet Woods   64

Alyssa R. Bernstein
Right Here in Athens 65
Brenda Jean Searcy
Pawpaw Tree 66
Byron Hoot
So Much Depends 67
Martha G. Michael
PawPawlicious 68
Meredith S. Jensen
Host Plant 69
Matt Peters
Haiku Triloba 71
Paul M. Noser
The Secret Fruit 72
Sydney Joslin-Knapp
Ohio Tropics 73
Emily Anderson
Ode to Pawpaw 74
Ohio's Native Fruit 75
Jay Hostetler
Pawpaw Trees 76
Pawpaw Trees 2 77
Natalie Burton
Pawpaws on Parade 78
Maeve Denshaw
Pawpaw Poem 79
Jennifer L'Heureux
Almighty Pawpaw 80
Ikaika Grimm
Untitled 3 81
Shei Sanchez
Dear Pawpaw, ... 82
Jessica Held
Pawpaw Stool 83
Jennifer Schomburg Kanke
Not All Pollinators Love Sweetness 84
I Scream, You Scream 85
Ikaika Grimm
Untitled 1 86
Diane Kendig
PAWPAWS 87
Jennifer Schwirian
Ode to Pawpaw 88

Tina Moore
Pawpaws   91
Cody Dikis
Scoop Eating   92
Martha G. Michael
Pawpaw   93
Southeastern Ohio   94
Haven Horton-Kunce
Maw Maw   95
Chelsea McClellan
I Consider Answering, but then, Refrain   96
Bonnie Proudfoot
Haibun with Pawpaws   97

Contributors   98

PREFACE

The North American pawpaw (Asimina triloba) is the largest native tree fruit on the continent. Its native range is twenty five states east of the Mississippi from Michigan to Florida. It has been growing here for over 30,000 years. So, why do so few people nowadays actually know what a pawpaw is, and why haven't more people enjoyed the delicious tropical flavored custard-like fruit of the pawpaw?

Back in history, the pawpaw provided for indigenous cultures and early frontier peoples. In the early 1900s, it was known as "the poor man's banana" and provided needed nutrition in the depression era. But as our agriculture, diet, technology, and economies changed, knowledge of and access to the pawpaw fruit withered. We mostly now just go to the store and buy what is presented on the grocery store shelves. We have plenty of avocados, bananas, citrus, and other fruits available year-round. These are all provided by the complex agricultural food system that spans the globe and leads to the statistic that every food calorie now requires up to fourteen fossil fuel calories to be produced. Or that the produce on your grocery store shelf travels 1,500 miles before it is consumed. This modern-day reality is why most people haven't had a pawpaw—it isn't on the grocery store shelf.

The pawpaw, a member of the Custard Apple Family, Annonaceae, is a very soft and perishable fruit. Though it can be picked slightly under ripe to be shipped, it has a very short shelf life. It does not age well. It goes from hard as a rock to over ripe and rotten in a matter of days. This reality does not blend well with our current food system that transports produce for thousands of miles. But if you are lucky enough to encounter a perfectly ripe pawpaw, you won't forget it. What an amazing flavor that you've never experienced before. The flavor can have hints of mango, bubblegum, or tropical paradise.

These challenges shaped our thought processes as young people. Believing in the motto of turning problems into solutions, we made the best of turning these challenges into opportunities for growth. For some reason, the Appalachian hills in Southeast Ohio seemed to be prolific in pawpaws. Producing abundantly, the pawpaw fruit laid on the ground, wasted. This led to the creation of the Ohio Pawpaw Festival. Why not celebrate the pawpaw and its obscurity and unavailability by hosting a festival? Why not turn these challenges into opportunities by educating folks about all the nuances of the pawpaw? How to grow it, how to eat it, how to judge it, how to cook with it, how to make beer with it, and how to celebrate it.

The Ohio Pawpaw Festival is a symbolic format for bringing pawpaw consciousness to the masses. That's why all this pawpaw art is so important. The creative power of people exploring, in their own ways, what pawpaws are and mean is pretty amazing. All the different people over the years, in their different mediums, have expressed the pawpaw. What is it? Why is it important? Art is so great at that.

The pawpaw is an ancient fruit that has modern appeal. That may be part of why the pawpaw has become such a symbol of nature for so many.

Chris Chmiel and Michelle Gorman
Founders of the Ohio Pawpaw Festival

I Searched For Your Sweetness

I searched for your sweetness
from Raccoon Creek to the Shenandoah's flow
I gathered enough of your delicacy
to fill the bottom of my boat

I smelled your perfume
in the light of warm September
I savored your taste
so long ago I barely remember

Roadside Searching

I'm in search of a tree's mystery,
Summer solstice, 2006, dreaming
I could find one last tree standing,

with my grandfather there digging
his thumbs into soft skin, peeling
back the olive green and scraping

the bright flesh with his upper teeth,
spitting out the seeds along the road,
me now hunting by ripening scent

memory, wondering if he'd started
this or that tree, seeking his shade.

A Communion

The simple act of breaking open fruit.
My grandfather balling his hands
around the halves of a large ripe pawpaw
he let me pick from a backyard tree,
his thumbnails pressing in
and breaking the flesh, rupturing
the mottled skin, mango-like yellow giving
and showing like sudden sun.
            The scent, instant, unmistakable
as a single event, even there where so many
ripening fruit filled the air. Him keeping a half,
he'd hand me the other, assuming I craved them
as he did.
            I was sometimes unsure if I liked them,
or if I only wanted to like them because he did,
which was good enough.

How could something so simple be wrong?

Pawpaw in Crayon
Crayon on paper: 7" x 5″, 2024
Albany, Ohio—Age 16

David B. Prather

Anthimeria Lover

I verb my way into your heart,
scatter mulberry adjectives

into your strawberry chambers.
I language your mouth

with all my synonyms for kiss,
even those I make up

with my loquacious lips.
I willow your skin, pawpaw

your flesh, pine your body
with mine. I sunlight your eyes.

I moonlight through leaves
to find you. When I ocean to you,

you coastline to my every touch.
Noun each thought, ripen them

real as berry and fruit, bittersweet
your teeth and tongue.

I honeysuckle my vines
around your wisteria limbs,

and we honeybee, hummingbird
each other. All night,

I cloud upon your river, clad
in humid air, rise, rise. And I

firefly with you, make stars
among the trees as gods whippoorwill

far away, even as we participle,
conjugate, and sway.

Originally published in *The Passionfruit Review*

Way Down Yonder

My great grandmother loved Burl Ives,
his jolly voice lifted
from vinyl grooves, blooming
from stereo speakers. Her favorite song

was one that reminded her of childhood
in the country where winding one-lane
roads got tangled up with streams

and snaked up hillsides.
I was a city boy who had to ask
what the lyrics meant—*way down yonder
in the pawpaw patch*. She promised

one day she would take me into the wild
to taste the *banango,* a word she made up
to make me want it more. She said

it was like walking back into Paradise,
but I think that was surely her longing
for the past, her memories of late summer
sun melted down between the leaves.

We had a honeyed history—her past,
my future, the brief time our lives
overlapped. Someone took her

music, all those old standards.
Someone else gathered her treasure
of photos. I hope they look through them
every now and again. And I hope

somewhere among those pictures
is one of her as a girl
stuffing her pockets full of pawpaws.

Appalachian RE: Revision

With belated gratitude to K.D.

Before I learned to lean into my Appalachian, I was just a
kid in the mountains who thought the osage oranges that
rolled down Pawpaw Way must be pawpaws, and when
we broke and ate one, there was no banana sweetness, no
silky custard, just a hard and spitting-bitter green. The
neighbor boys threw the other monkey balls at passing
cars and ran. The chemical and tire plants closed, cancer
rose like mill-steam, and I ran from cast iron, too,
preferred awhile the slip of nonstick Calphalon, postured
in a flattened, formal English-major voice, but when a
lanky beauty of a bad-for-me man slid a sautéed leaf of
pigweed onto my tongue, showed me hollers I had never
seen, I learned to look at field guides, to gather ramps and
forage chanterelles, pack duxelles into a winter freezer
beside quarts of swamp-sweet blueberries. I doubled up
my nouns and dropped infinitives, finally told friends
about my cousin's meth, great-grandad's still explosion,
about the horse thief hanging in the family tree, slurped at
bowls of greens and soup beans with gratitude like water,
leaned. I've learned to look for gentleness, for north-facing
slopes, can tell, of course, a pawpaw from an osage orange,
have figured in the bitterness how to make things smooth,
how to make them sweet.

Patricia Thrushart

Lewis & Clarke Survive on Pawpaw, 1806

You are on your way home.
The deer are lean and meager,
the biscuits nearly gone.

You feel your hunger grow, your gut twist.
Someone knows a tree with an ugly fruit,
growing in the low bottom woods,
along the streams that feed the river.

You find its excess on the ground
quick to rot as the humid hours pass,
returning to the flies
who first sipped its flower.

You cut through the spotted skin
along the bulbous length,
scoop out the pulpy flesh
that yields without protest.

You didn't know to take
no scrap of skin or seed,
lest they sicken you.
And they do,
as the sweet juice drips from your lips
to your calloused hands,
then inflames your weary homesick eyes
when you rub them,
because you can take no more,
because they have seen too much.

Katarena Altier

Cycle of the Pawpaw
Autodesk Sketchbook: 8"x 8", 2024
Athens, Ohio

Jennifer Browne

Fourteen*

The seeds in sphagnum in my crisper drawer
are not pawpaws, though they may grow to
trees if I don't fail at any of the stages when
things might fail, germination, shading slow
saplings. If they grow to be as tall as men,
they may fruit, if stigmas aren't unpollinated
(bee loss, perils in the atmosphere). I imagine
their eventual weight in my hands, though
this cold-fogged ziplock is hardly fertile soil.
We who bleed know that anything can happen,
the silent cells that wait within our bodies are
just cells, whatever they might become, how
they might pulse later. A seed is not fruit, not
the tree. A seed is not sweetness in the mouth.

*A pawpaw bears 10-14 seeds per fruit. Fourteen US states
have recently considered fetal personhood bills.*

Kari Gunter-Seymour

Pawpaws Are Ripe

Bumper crop, enough to sate taste buds,
skins split open on the spot, pulp scooped
fingers-to-mouth, the rest collected
for sweet breads, hand-churned ice cream,

home brewed beer. I smile at all the ways
my people have come to preserve
this delicate fruit, one of the few treasures
of this ridge not yet stripped or clear cut,

fragrant like a ripe banana, hints
of strawberry, pineapple, mango,
flesh creamy yellow, spicy
brown seeds—same sown centuries ago

by Shawnee, Delaware and Mingo.
Once a year I harvest, render, reflect,
return seeds to native soil, on my knees,
every turn of the trowel a benediction.

Originally published in *Dirt Songs* (Eastover Press)

Tom Barlow

Orphans

The orphan cuts school again
to hide from her tormentors
deep in the hollow where she is
surrounded by only peace. She

feels safe there on a tract of land
so useless to the dozers and drills
even a lone pawpaw has survived,
a tree waiting in vain year after year

for the black bear and his appetite
to spread its seeds. The orphan runs
her hand across its rare bark, grabs
one of the ripe fruit and as she tears

it open and scoops out the pulp
with her fingers she both pities
the tree that it cannot run away
when confronted by violent men

and envies the pawpaw that it has
never been ordered to pack up its
sparse belongings and get in the car.
Instead the fruit has grown in this

quiet isolation for hundreds of years,
yet continues to convey hope for
more of its kind with every flower.
Touched by this rare constancy,

the orphan carefully picks out the seeds
and gathers them in a tissue, vows she
will plant them all when she finds
a forever home and the two of them
will never be lonely again.

Fenestrated

oak leaves, or maple,
marijuana's mournful fingers
reach for me in the dark,
gunera or ferns,
food for dinosaurs,
and us, fiddle head
eaters, weed-smokers,

acorn people. With clusters
of pink seed heads and dried pods
of poppy from a neighbour's garden.
where do I look between the parted

ways, the veering outwards, and up.
Sit here with me, home, I call it,
to heed pawpaw of the midwestern
type, three years and still
stunted, slow growing—two

for pollination, the leaves unbroken,
oblong, not fenestrated,
but I will wait with them,
simple, yellow,
a bit desiccated,
anticipate the fruit,
bound, or armored
in oval shell,
hidden, only edible
when ripe, tropical

flavor, mango, banana,
almost forgotten,
once megafauna,
food for mammoths, mastadons,

and even, lewis and clark,
with roots that sucker
through our clay beds,
this one is a survivor.

Anna Robinson

Pawpaw
Oil painting on canvas board: 5″ x 7″, 2022
Ferndale, Michigan

What I Saw Under the Pawpaw Tree

I sat at the base of the Pawpaw tree
I thought about everything that I could see
An ovenbird
Was all I heard
A slimy snail
Left a shiny trail
While a Zebra Swallowtail
Flew past a spicebush
I see a wolf spider push
Through the layered leaves
I feel a light breeze
The bluebells bend from bumblebees
Ginseng grows beneath a hickory
A cherry millipede crawls near the sweet cicely
Deer graze on the edge of the forest
The peepers sing a continuous chorus
I fall asleep to the sound of the stream
Tasting the pawpaw in my dream
Soon I awaken
From a cool wind that has shaken
The fruit loose and falling
A cluster lands nearby, it's calling
Eat me
So I do
The taste exceeds
My wildest dreams
A hint of banana
Coconut and mango
Passion fruit and papaya
But above all else
It tastes like a pawpaw
That soft yellow flesh tastes so sweet
I even cleaned it right off of the seeds
Spitting them out hoping they grow
Saving them too late to sow

I pick up the extras and put them in a sack
I make my way back
To the Pawpaw Festival
Where I will tell
Everyone I see
What I saw under the pawpaw tree

Pawpaw Ice Cream
Marker on paper: 8.5″ x 11″, 2024
Nelsonville, Ohio—Age 10

Kristine Williams

Bombs for Pawpaws

Last week,
I was angry for days,
because animals beat me
to most of the pawpaws growing
at the edge of the yard.

I am on my knees
while bombs fall in Israel.

I gather the remaining pawpaws,
each soft as a peach,
to make jam,
while bombs fall in Israel.

I am on my knees.
How dare I complain?

Later,
I walk with my husband,
hand wrapped securely in his,
while across an ocean,
a woman holds the cooling hand
of her child,
on her knees,
while bombs fall.

How the size of the world
shrinks
to the size of the tragedies
we survive.

January in Athens County

Days of cold
and snow
and quiet
lead to contemplative thoughts
of deer
under the pawpaw tree,
and how
even though the days
grow longer,
it feels darker—
clouds clog the sky,
grey against lighter grey,
snow falls,
the hush
felt in our bones,
how the wind
tightens the flesh
over cheekbones,
thin already,
now burning.

A piece of toast,
the last jar of pawpaw jam,
smelling of summer,
all that anchors me
most days.

Bon appétit!

Pawpaws have never sung
to me, although I love
wandering in the woods
under their fan-like leaves,
perhaps while eating a peach.

One year at the Pawpaw
Festival, someone thought
it would be a good idea to toss
pawpaw slurry on the ground
in front of the stage.
Dancers bold — or stoned —
enough to leap, dive, spin
into that space, impelled
by sunshine and an insistent
beat, slipped and slid
in the fragrant mud.
That did it for me.

My friend made a pawpaw pie
after her eager daughter brought
a full basket home from the woods.
"Mama, let's make a pie!"
So they did. Just that once.

I have a wary affection
for pawpaws, native fruit
of our Appalachian woods,
but please leave them there,
for squirrels and raccoons
to savor.

Pawpaw popsicles?
Pawpaw salsa?
Thanks, I'll pass.

Bon appétit!

Renee Williams

Mangoes in the Mist

I didn't believe him.
Mangoes, he said. *Mangoes,*
right up on the hillside
behind the house.

Mangoes. Time,
limited, and maybe
he knew. Autumn approached,
gentle winds, chilling
temperatures. Leaving us
would be his only option.

Eighty-three and stubborn,
ever the farm boy who knew
his way around a garage
and now, humbled by strokes,
heart attacks, even heart
failure, he found himself

taking more pills than he could count
and sometimes, heaven
help us, he was seeing
or accused of seeing things
that weren't there, like the strangers
in the neighbor's truck

or the ants on the floor,
leading one nurse to suggest
guns be taken out of the house,
though we kept finding them, hidden

in his recliner, under the bed, in jacket pockets.
He was so weak,
could hardly walk across the floor,

needing a cane but only submitting
to a wheelchair for doctor appointments
if then. One day after making
this declaration, he scooted away,
while no one was looking,

while my mother walks with her dog,
trying to carve out some piece
of sanity for herself without
his incessant demands, and by the grace
of the Almighty, he managed

to climb that hill and procure
that mango, being assisted
back down the hill
when a kindly neighbor saw him.

Triumphant grin, those blue-green eyes
that matched my own dancing, he reached
for my hand, dropping
the prize upon me. *Mango,*
he proclaimed.

Squeezing that pawpaw
gently, fighting back tears,
I gazed at him, maybe knowing
even then we had just weeks.

Mango, I said.

Sherry Deskins Goodson

Juno Beach, Florida Pawpaw Bloom
Watercolor: 9" x 12", 2024
Palm Beach Shores, Florida

Roses are Red

Roses are red,
Violets are blue,
I love pawpaws,
And so should you.

Here in Bismarck, North Dakota

How I wish I could plant myself a pawpaw tree,
Here in Bismarck, North Dakota.
Yet I know all too well that I live in Zone Three,
Here in Bismarck, North Dakota.
If ever global warming comes into this place,
Here in Bismarck, North Dakota.
I could plant myself a pawpaw tree in this space,
Here in Bismarck, North Dakota.
Should I gamble that my home will become Zone Five,
Here in Bismarck, North Dakota?
With the warming that methane flaring can contrive,
Here in Bismarck, North Dakota?
So it's will I or won't I, sitting on the fence,
Here in Bismarck, North Dakota.
To plant asimina trees or use common sense,
Here in Bismarck, North Dakota.

Jean Mikhail

There, You'll Find Them

In that field, beyond abandoned
barn, a pitchfork shadow leans,
an antique hay baler, too,
has given up the ghost, gone
to rust out in the moon's
magnetic field. On that land,
you'll find the pawpaw trees.
They are out past the sagging barn,
more stooped than it used to be,
but the barn door still gives,

just lift the latch a little.
I used to climb into the loft, my heart
throat-pounding as I ascended
into the heavenly breeze,
when I found myself to be
the proud owner of a small farm
at the Jesus-age of 33.
I owned the farmhouse,
barn, surrounding fields,
and a pond, and you

remained there with me
for awhile to grow
to love, too, the enormous
barn dwarfing the house,
where humongous rats ran,
and mouser cats never
lived up to their name. Adding
insult to injury, a rat snake
once curled behind
a wall next to my bed.

I stayed there for over
five years, but had no

business living there.
I did not work the soil.
I let the fields go fallow,
sprouting with scrubby trees.
I clotheslined in the yard, pinned
my fanny to the porch swing,
fished the pond, braved
snapping turtles and tried

to mend the fence surrounding
the pasture beyond the pond.
That is where I discovered them:
pawpaw trees, ungainly fruit
dropping, small, green
like a misshapen potato. My heart
double-timed when I found
out what they were, pawpaws,
and that I could eat all

I wanted to for free. I landed
on my knees to collect them
from the ground, then turned
around to see those ghosts
wanting something, too.
Maybe they were the souls
of children I'd never have with you.

Through bromegrass, they floated
as gracefully as they came,
thrusting out their hay hands
surrendering them to the horses.
They headed down the windy road,
graveled over, their voices
carrying to the edges of the field
where they stopped to feed
the neighbor's black mare.

I never saw them again.
I can't explain how I saw
the unseeable, fully present.

Then cross words came between us.
I took a wrong turn down that road
maybe for the worse. You left me,
or maybe I left you. I found
a place with fewer ghosts,

but my heart remained
heavy, green with envy,
for those who now owned
the pawpaw trees
on my old property,
the new farm occupants,
swimmers of the pond,
pluckers of the gooseberries,
basketers of pawpaws.
Those souls who tended
to the vines of strange
white flowers that opened
when the moon's magnet pulled
them in all directions,
up a trellis to the roof.
They seemed to fly.

I don't know the names
of many trees or flowers,
but I came to recognize
the pawpaw trees, and the sweet
fruit that never needs tending,
that produces fruit whether
rain comes, heavy or not
heavy. They drop their dry blood
blooms before bursting in fruit
of honeydew moon, cantaloupe sun,
a touch of peach, nearly turned,
a cross between sweetness,
and sweetness withheld.

Softening

Fermented? Rotten?
Past ripeness not yet spoiled —
bletted fruit, pawpaws.

Katherine Ziff

Good Morning
Woodcut print: 11.5" x 11.5", 2016
Athens, Ohio

When do you pick pawpaws?
They say you don't.
They say to stand there and
catch them when they fall.

Here's my story of falling pawpaws

We moved from Morris Avenue
where we planted a row of evergreens,
roses,
and a pink dogwood.

To the North Ridge
where I cleared brush
our first winter.

Fall came
chilly crisp.

What is this?
Stones have fallen
in the night!

Looking closely
I saw I had a pawpaw patch to tend.

Planting Pawpaws

Their seeds look like coat buttons smeared
in the fallen fruit's ripe custard.
Pushing four of them into compost pots
in fall for planting is a category of defiance,
a confidence that seasons and shadows,
sunlight when it comes, will be kind,
that life will limb into sturdy bones,
that bones will leaf and bloom, and blooms
expand to fruit settlers here called
Hillbilly Banana, or Quaker Delight.
A complicated sweetness that surprises
in a season when everything else is dying.
My therapist friend says you can talk yourself
into hope, a new life, but it's work
to force something bright from a dark place,
like searching the woods for a fruit tree
that bends between borders and wastelands.
A neighbor gave me a bucket of them,
and I spoon the pulp, seeds and all,
directly into my mouth, smooth
the small stones with my tongue and spit
them into my palm. Some may rot
in the planter, may be scavenged
by squirrels or broken by ice in winter,
but if I'm lucky, if all the promises nature makes
with fingers crossed and eyebrows furrowed,
then one day I'll lift ripe pawpaws
off the ground and give you some.

Originally published in *Cultural Daily*

Rebekah Cotton

How to Make Pawpaw Pudding

Before you round up some butter, sugar, milk, and flour,
head out to the four pawpaw trees by the pond,
the trees your dad planted back when he was planting fruit trees
and eating pawpaws. Pick the pawpaws off the ground

(*never off the trees*!), the ones with black spots are A-OK,
don't grip too tight or SPLAT. Give them a wash-off
in the kitchen sink, peel carefully—*don't waste fruit!*—
and wow look at that pale orange flesh

that takes you back to when you and your dad
were walking home after collecting those first pawpaws,
back to when he rubbed that splotchy fruit on his T-shirt,
held it up to his wide-open mouth and bit straight through the skin

into that pastel flesh, his eyes closed in delight.
That was the best pawpaw in the history of pawpaws,
he said. *Did you know pawpaws are excellent*
for papas but also for mamas and their urchin?

He tossed an oval fruit your way and what could you do
but follow his lead? Of course you spit out the bitter skin—
but that sweet juice dribbling down your chin:
mango, banana, pear?

In a few years there'll be more pawpaws
than a family could ever hope for. Wouldn't it be nice
to make some pawpaw pudding? Fact is you never made
pawpaw pudding, not in all those 50 years since,

and now when you head out to those four trees,
you realize they aren't dropping fruit like in your dad's day.
There's nothing for it but to special-order
some frozen pawpaw pulp, an arm and two legs' worth,

but it's A-OK because it happens to be your dad's birthday
and even now you want to do right by him so you thaw
the fruit and grease the old Corning Ware,
measure, and whisk—*genuine vanilla required,*

fresh chicken eggs preferred—and when it's baked
and cooled, you center it on a fancy tablecloth, poke
a lighted candle in the middle, sing the birthday song,
and laugh out loud when that first spoonful hits your
wide-open mouth.

Pawpaw
Ceramic tile
Mechanicsburg, Ohio

Pawpaw Trees in Winter

Diaphanous cold.
Lime and magenta
waiting to flower.

Breathing beings
inhale and transform.
Tea green and golden sweet.

Chris Farrell

A Pawpaw Prayer

A cold freeze came and killed my trees.
So I prayed to God and asked him, "Please,
Give me a fruit that resists the cold
And will live for years 'till I get old;
That I might eat of the fruit of that tree.
(Not to be confused with Eve! Oh, no! Not me!)
But just to make some Jelly or Jam,
Some Pudding to go with Green Eggs and Ham!"

The Lord responded, "Pawpaw's pretty good.
George Washington loved it just as you should!
The Indians too liked the wrinkly fruit,
And it grows real nice down there in the Boot
Where Cajuns push their pirogues by
The pawpaw pollinated by the fly
Because its flowers smell like 'sheet.'
You'd better plant it down the street!"

Consider the Pawpaw

I begin to think
about pawpaws
when spring flowers
open on the hillsides
in a rainbow welcoming
warm weather and
sunshine as we rise
from the depths of
ice storms and blizzards
that tipped up trees
and carved their memory
into the forest.
I gather morels and watch
trillium unfold, petals so white
they make the steepest cliffs
look snow-covered in April.
Then, I know pawpaw
flowers will be waking
in the understory,
blooming as the
redbuds and dogwoods
steal the show,
but the true beauty bears
not just pretty petals, but
also a delicacy
come September.

Ars Pawpaw

Let words come out lush like ripe
pawpaws fallen for hungry opossums,

sweet scent wafting through the forest air so thick
it's all you can smell at peak season.

Let them bleed onto the page
pouring out your heart right there,

taking root like emerging seedlings
weaving meaning from heartaches and joys

as tangled as those knotted, weblike roots
pushing their way down deep into dirt.

Growing sturdy and strong like tree trunks on the page,
layering new rings each year,

though they only look like rings when we cut them down,
cross sectioning their histories,

learning their life stories told in thickness and thinness,
the ebbing and flowing of water and nutrients,

fire scars, and insect tunnels,
examining whole forests for their fruits, waiting,

watching them grow tougher with time,
branches into the sky,

trees emerging from seeds like words from the pen,
reaching for more.

L.D. Nehls

Northside Neighbors
Digital Illustration/Mural 9" x 12", 2023
Cincinnati, Ohio

Jeri Kendrick

Pawpaws

Soft fruit with black seeds
full of healthy vitamins
Athens festival

Tie-dyed shirt and jeans
sipping on pawpaw smoothies
I miss my hippies.

Jennifer Michelle Mayer

Asimina

Soft yellow teardrop, pawpaw leaf
gently laid along a forearm, elbow to pulse.
We search for the bulge of full fruit in late summer,
branches hung ripe where spring blossoms once
opened brown-maroon for pollinator friends.

At fall, we caw-caw in the grassroots festival—
the fruit grows community in Appalachian hills.
We praise this native named a regional pride,
propagate in honor of indigenous roots,
cloning itself resilient in the understory.

We join with hands that scooped golden flesh
from green skins, made barter and beads
ages after mastodons roamed Ohio land
masticating custard pulp, spreading
rich seeds for tomorrow, today.

Pawpaw, Reversed

Plant. Propagate.
Revive. Germinate.
Stratify. Overwinter.
Pack with peat to keep damp and cold.
Dormant. Loop with clay or agate.
Drill holes for earrings.
Decorate. Dry some.
Save the seeds.
Scrape remains over framed screens.
Ferment for festival beer.
Purée for pancake batter, ice cream.
Dice for salsa, smash for sauce.
Savor from the spoon, carefully scooped.
Custard fruit, custard flesh. Cut in two.
Don't consume the thick, toxic peel.
Spare a few for tasting.
Share with raccoons.
Shake a slender trunk, gather fresh.
Caw: pawpaw, pawpaw!
Call to the gathering.
Sing the Pawpaw Song.
Early autumn. Over, summer.

That Underappreciated Fruit

O - Lovely pawpaw
Ohio grown
West Virginia, also known
Your soft, green skin
So fragile and bright
Your sweet, fruit aroma
I smell at night
Those big, smooth seeds, so fun for crafts
Hunting pawpaws, is such a blast
There's so much out there
The earth provides
Go find some pawpaws
And get outside

Pawpaw1
Oil on canvas: 11" x 14",2022
Athens, Ohio

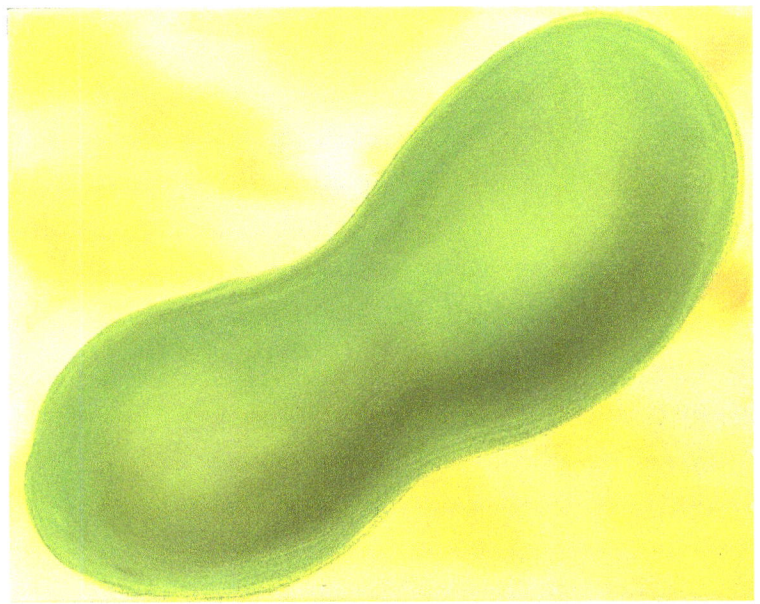

A Brief History of the Pawpaw

We can never realize what a great blessing the pawpaw was to the first settlers while they were clearing the great natural forest and preparing to build cabins.

—James A. Little (1905)

Water clouded memories   of tramping through
poplar coated forests   to the mountain top
of grandma's farm   seeking a holy grail
of greenish-blackish delight

discovered by Spanish conquistadors   saving Lewis and Clark
feeding Shawnees   during their special month
enjoyed by George Washington and Thomas Jefferson
hard-farming pioneers   singing its praises

the western swing rainbow   of Asleep at the Wheel
reverberant through   the hollers' reminiscences
from a namesake burg

drowning in irrelevance   of folksy nicknames
like Indian banana   custard apple   Quaker delight

until resuscitated   in a groundswell renaissance
ripping into the skin   right there on the hilltop
slurping the pulp   spitting out the seeds
in rapturous gooeyness.

Jessica Weyer-Bentley

The Sage Witness

When the sun caresses the mountain valley,
meet me beneath our pawpaw tree,
where the black slate headstones stand resolute in silent
    declaration.
Let us pry upon their whispered history,
as the creek sweeps their secrets over moss burdened stone.
We will climb the fragrant branches,
among the flora of burgundy,
shielding our union until the sun bids farewell to the moon.
Fear will give way to Faith,
vowing to avoid the somber pitfalls of these epitaphs.
Palm in palm,
a cadent breath with breath,
the foothills will stand guard once more,
as our weary frames lean into our rough aging witness.

Jason Baldinger

in an elk's eye

found myself in an elk's eye
green emerald and brown water
roll muskingum roll

another dead possum highway
another canned goods library
here in the black diamond
spring turns to summer
in bee balm and fresh turned earth

the heart of an appalachian highway
foothills colonized in buckeye and pawpaw
with a deep enough breath
you smell miners' bones mouldering
you smell the death of cilia
you smell operators rooting
through generations of robbery
turns out oppression and pitch
smell exactly the same

the little scioto is a faun
morning sun chokes on afternoon clouds
the ancient art of alchemy
here the adena learned to brand
snakes into the earth
a letter to the dead
an arrow from the heavens

la belle riviere throws back the sun
this meandering topography
read as a dog-eared pulp novel
the plot threaded through a needle
this is what humans leave behind

under a pawpaw

the armadillo heaves
a heavy sigh
at the next and
last state line
step right up
appalachia is waiting again

haggard after
skywriting figure eights
across the Midwest

if you need me
I'll be under a
pawpaw
a bed of leaves
constellations of seed pods
the cusp of a season
waiting like a fool
for ripe fruit
to fall

L.D. Nehls

Evolutionary Anachronisms of Burnet Woods
(American Persimmon, Pawpaw, and Ground Sloth)
Acrylic paint on panel: 8" x 8", 2021
Cincinnati, Ohio

Alyssa R. Bernstein

Right Here in Athens

I overheard a college student say to her friend
"Wikipedia says a pawpaw is a papaya"
What? I am not a papaya!
I am nowhere near as big,
as hard on the digestive system,
as unsubtly flavored
as any kind of papaya.

But Wikipedia says I am.
So now lots of people,
maybe billions,
think I'm a papaya.

Does that mean I am? No.
"Perception is reality," but it's not true.

What if I can't change their minds?
They won't be able to understand me,
really know me, appreciate me.

But all you need is love,
as the immortal Beatles sang.

All you need is true love,
true friendship, or true appreciation
by the person who really knows you.

And right here in Athens, Ohio,
many people know that I'm a pawpaw,
not a papaya,
and some of them
really appreciate me.

Pawpaw Tree

Years ago, I broke the earth and blessed it with a song.
I took a tiny seedling, placed it right where it belonged.
I nurtured it with all my heart, my precious, growing tree.
And I waited patiently…
For the luscious fruit from off my pawpaw tree.

Years you'd grown together, then I happened by your way.
Like the fragrance of a flower, your lover took my breath away.
Unwittingly exuding beauty wafting on the air.
And my heart lay open, bare…
So she paused to hold me in my agony.

I dreamed that I could love her and that your love would remain;
That such a boundless vessel all our passions could contain!
I saw the rings, and then I saw desire in her eyes
That she could not justify…
So the consummation never was to be.

The Mighty Storm, the Fury, the chrysalis torn apart.
I did not understand the burning rage from out your heart.
I'd never seen the eyes of hatred staring into me.
Then a thought occurred to me…
I would fight like hell to save my pawpaw tree.

But a woman's not a creature you can plant like tree or vine.
And a woman is possessed of her own heart and soul and mind.
She is neither mine nor yours; how frightening it must be!
So go on and rage at me…
As alone I gaze upon my pawpaw tree.

So Much Depends

I thought Pawpaw was my grandpa.
At seven or eight my mom
gave me a spoonful – she said, "Paw—
paw. It's good for you."
And I replied, "Pawpaw"
and gabbed our fishing poles.

Martha Gallagher Michael

PawPawlicious
Gel plate acrylic monoprint: 8" x 10", 2024
Columbus, Ohio

Host Plant

Who knows the zebra swallowtail?
Who recognizes its spring and summer morphs?
Who shades the color of its sky-blue spots, the underwing
  red that pools on its outer margin?
Who traces the black-and-white stripes of its stained-glass
  scales?
Who understands the eponymous "tails" of its hindwings
  are not a tail at all?

Who knows the zebra swallowtail?
Who puts out its maroon, double-tricorn flowers as a first
  food source?
Who pushes from its branches subtropical leaves, the
  winter buds once used as paintbrushes?
Who pumps those leaves with toxic acetogenins to ward
  off defoliating insects?
Who sets the dappled sunlight of spring's Appalachian
  understory?

Who knows the zebra swallowtail?
Who feels when an over-wintered female alights upon its
  branches, tasting with her feet?
Who senses when she curls her body and oviposits,
  touching her abdomen to bark and bud?
Who cradles these eggs, just one for each leaf to avoid
  larval cannibalism?
Who watches them hatch after four to ten days?

Who knows the zebra swallowtail?
Who complements the caterpillars' green, white, blue, and
  black stripes?
Who provides the toxic salad bar that makes them bitter
  poison, protecting them from predation?
Who shelters them through their life stages, called instars,
  over three to four weeks?

Who sees them off to pupate into their leaf-mimic chrysalis
held to a twig with silk?

Who knows the zebra swallowtail?
Who welcomes the newly eclosed adults after two weeks or
an entire winter?
Who drops its summer-ripe fruit for males to puddle on,
sucking up vital minerals and nutrients?
Who rejoices when two fluttering bodies dance together for
the next generation?
Who mourns this butterfly when it dies after one precious
week of life?

Who knows the zebra swallowtail?
Who knows everything it needs and needs everything it
knows?
Who is the only plant that can support its caterpillars, the
sole host of an entire species?
Who has nurtured this relationship for nigh on millions of
years?
Who is *Asimina triloba*, the pawpaw tree?

Haiku Triloba

flies buzz lazily
in the shade of the glade where
I fill my pawchets

big pawpaws sweet with
all summer long sunshine and
heavy with the rains

these pawpaw trees grow
thick among the hickory
and silent oaks here.

Paul M. Noser

The Secret Fruit

Leaves so smooth and large
Are they really from the tropics
No they are very much at home
Wherever they are grown

No other trees around
Seem to hide from all
Unknown by most who seek
To be aware of the surround

Early autumn brings a hurry
Sweeten and fill with seeds
A fruit like no other
Shied by so many its form

So many takers around in woods
The morsels won't last for long
Some get picked from the tree
Any that fall will surly please

The savory fruit that resides
All around the curious seeds
Will make for even ice cream
The brave is rewarded no doubt
The strange and secretive
Pawpaw will please

Sydney Joslin-Knapp

Ohio Tropics
Paint pen & colored pencil on card stock 8" x 10", 2023
Dayton, Ohio

Ode to Pawpaw

Behold, a fruit with green skin,
and a white-yellow creamy pulp within.
Flowers of maroon show in the spring,
signifying the joy this fruit will bring.

Containing 10 to 20 bean-shaped seeds,
it often gets lost in the weeds.
Fruits for harvest in late August to mid-October
but that does not mean the party is over.

Ohio's Native Fruit

The Native Fruit of Ohio
is very hard to buy-o.
It has a short season,
So that may be the reason.
That's why you need to attend the Pawpaw Fest of Ohio.

Pawpaw Trees
Pawpaw wood: Heights vary 6" to 15", 2023
Athens, Ohio

Jay Hostetler

Pawpaw Trees 2
Pawpaw wood: vary 6" to 15", 2023
Athens, Ohio

Natalie Burton

Pawpaws on Parade

Yippie Skippie
It's that time of year
When pawpaws come out to play
Rolling and cajoling
Yellow Plump Wee Womblies
Scattering across the ground
Squishy Squashy memories
Pawpaws on Parade

Custard apple friendships
Buttery velvet delicious bits
Slipping through my fingertips
Dancing your way into bliss
Pawpaws on Parade

Bananas, mangos, or melons
Haven't got a shot
Cause the pawpaw got what they ain't got
Your yummy tummy flavor is so divine
Love this Ohio native
You are so freakin' fine
Vibin' melody of juiciness
Tasty bites of happiness
Float on down
Into
My
Mouth
Cheer! Hooray!!
Pawpaws on Parade

Pawpaw Poem

Happiness is like a pawpaw.
Sometimes it is found unexpectedly,
But it always seems right on time.

After looking in every grove,
After checking under every leaf,
There it is.

Right where you were meant to find it.

It's beautiful green skin,
It's imperfect lumps and bumps.

You knew it would be there.
A friendship that goes way back,
The pawpaw is just as happy to see you.

Almighty Pawpaw

Thank you Pawpaw
For having long, pretty leaves
On the end of your branches
That hide the fruit to feed the deer
And the special treats for those we hold near.

Thank you Pawpaw
For the complexity of your form
Your original shapes and
The color of your skin
And for the longing to find you
Each year again

Thank you Pawpaw
For your tasty pulp in your
Butters and jams, your beers and your dishes
Filling up our souls and
Satisfying downhome wishes.

For many years your seeds they flourish
Over trials of weather
And manmade challenges that test
Creatures and nature still
You provide nutrition, admiration and awe
Thank you, thank you Almighty Pawpaw.

Untitled 3
Watercolor: 8.5" x 5.5", 2024
Millfield, Ohio—Age 10

Dear Pawpaw,

You tasted like San Juan summers ago.
When narrow streets squinted from the sun
and a familiar texture lay on my tongue.
Ma said it was breadfruit. You loved it
when you were little, she winked.
You tasted like monsoon rain.
Banana leaves dripped heavy with August
and a custard apple lay in my hand.
From my bungalow, I listened to the sky
pour itself into the Andaman Sea.
I am changing my life, I said to the world.
The fruit's soft bumps pressed against my palm
when I ripped it open. For the first time,
I tasted freedom. Seasons passed
and I had forgotten you in the same way
I had forgotten myself. But somehow,
you remembered. Somehow,
you remembered when I found you
in the woods, gathered you
like fallen memories. With every creamy bite,
I tasted what I had lost.

Pawpaw Stool
Acrylic & oil paint, resin on wood stool: 12" x 12" x 29",
2023 Athens, Ohio

Jennifer Schomburg Kanke

Not All Pollinators Love Sweetness

When spring has come to the hill
and honeysuckle fills the air,
joy and pollinators
buzz by on impossible wings.
We hope for honey sweet
and apples in the fall.
Good friends, good bees,
may your colonies stay strong.
But what of the fly?
Annoyance, pest, unclean.
A swatter in every room,
a zapper on the porch,
as if they haven't a job to do,
as if those highfalutin' bees
would go anywhere near
a pawpaw tree.

Jennifer Schomburg Kanke

I Scream, You Scream

Y'all need to stop
saying these taste like
a banana. It's like
you're trying to sell people
something you think
they might not
otherwise buy.
The pawpaw
don't need
any of your pity,
all it needs
is some spiceberries
and a spoon…
and maybe
a little sugar…
and some milk…
but that ain't much,
not much at all.

Untitled 1
Watercolor: 8.5" x 5.5", 2024
Millfield, Ohio—Age 10

The wild cat protects the paw paws, so he can eat them to survive in his wild forest.

Diane Kendig

PAWPAWS

The fruit attracts…the beautiful zebra swallowtail butterfly.
—L.S.U. Online Ag Center

Maroon bells hang from palms
as wide as Rachmaninoff's reach
on these trees that are clonal, like Dolly,
so though a patch seems like many
way down yonder, it may be just one,
that onliest number, but must be two
to do its magic, dropping green globes
splotched with black continents, inside
a creamy sweetness as pocked with openings
as an old brain's lost memories
and pitted with mahogany knobs, big
as the top button on a coat's cowl-neck
that you undo to scoop this wild native fruit.

Originally published in *Derailleur Press*

Jennifer Schwirian

Ode to Pawpaw

Down in the holler
Where nobody goes
Far from the freeway
A place no one trolls.

The still creek guides me,
O'er rocks and downed trees,
Searching for sweetness
Only she gives me.

Deep in this holler
In the shade of oaks,
An underdog thrives.
A hunger evokes.

Nature's resilient,
Amazing and free;
Thickets and bushes
And one special tree.

Peace in this holler.
These woods are my church.
The birds, God's chorus;
They sing from their perch.

Beauty spellbinding.
The air smells like earth.
Purity here like
The dawn of my birth.

Hope in this holler.
Gifts she holds for me,
Foxes, black bears, birds,
Nobody and thee.

Only gravel roads
No hurry to rush.
Just me, my purpose -
So deep in this brush

Love in this holler
For secrets she holds
Searching for riches
I'm eager and bold.

Finding her treasure
While the birds sing soul.
Moving further in…
I can see my goal.

Joy in this holler!
My treasured pawpaw,
Poor man's banana,
I hold it with awe.

My hunger so strong.
My mouth dry with thirst.
Praise to the pawpaw
My happiness bursts.

Blessed for this holler.
A place no one plays.
I bend to one knee;
I could stay for days.

Her silence is thick.
The birds have moved on.
The trees surround me;
I may stay till dawn.

Cheers to the pawpaw!
So sweet and so fine.
You must agree, sir,
It is quite divine.

Down in the holler
Where nobody goes
Far from the freeway
A place no one trolls.

The pawpaw grows there
With little fanfare…
Shhhhhh…Please…
Don't ask me to share.

Pawpaws

Pawpaw is a fruit and it grows on a tree

You can make all different kinds of things with pawpaws

They even have a pawpaw festival in September
for people to come to

They have all different kinds of food
made with pawpaws

and crafts

They even have songs
about pawpaws.

Scoop Eating
Digital art: 1620 x 2160 pixels, 2024
Albany, Ohio—Age 16

Pawpaw

At summer's close in the
depths of the forest by
hand drawn paths in Albany, Ohio
that are really just established game trails
shadows seem to find the dried parts
and yellows splash the trees
and some of the tallest trees
closing in like dark clouds sometimes do
when storms come
hover at dusk
and there is a sense of the result of heaven and hell
palpable parts of the myths we have been
brought up on
the downpour eventually reaching and
drenching each and every one
of us

Then with gratitude we see the last of the fruit
sequestered like a jury
until the moment of verdict
heavy with juice
as sweet as baby breath
and ready to forgive
from the first
to the last bite.

Southeastern Ohio

Filling in the steps leaves
have already made
swollen with last night's rain
I breathe in the sanctity of pine
as perfume from God's
embalmed air
close my eyes to feel
sunlight walk carefully
on my back
as it anoints my beliefs
when rain water drips upon me
from above

to where I wander
finding nothing out of place
ferns at my knees
stones underneath
pawpaws dangling above
as green and as perfect as a wish
for a bluebird to appear
in the openness of a hidden meadow
deep inside an Albany forest,
and then I hear a bluebird call
keeping me present
and forever grateful
for this moment
in shade.

Maw Maw
Acrylic on canvas: 18" x 24"
Athens, OH

I Consider Answering, but then, Refrain

What a child digs for is his own possession;
what is poured into his ear, like the idle song of a pleasant singer,
floats out as lightly as it came in, and is rarely assimilated.
                                        ——Charlotte Mason

Ashwaghanda, only hardy to zone seven,
must be harvested by fall, but the stubborn
hopeful child still alive within me left one
standing there, as if zone six were southern,
there, where her bare feet ran to first,
where the pale red and wrinkled berry, squeezed
between her thumb and pointing finger, birthed
a hundred seeds — *Shawaganga babies!* —
if you asked her. My clear delight sparked
in her a change — now, she is my orchard guide,
apple, plum, it died, chamomile, shawaganga,
Mommy, this one is the Pawpaw tree! With pride,
I think, *Why am I so surprised by her memory?*
She thinks, then asks me, *Where's the MawMaw tree?*

Haibun with Pawpaws

If a day had a color, the color would be gold: leaves of hickory, walnut, poplar stippling high branches, tassels of oatgrass, light striping the lawn. I could go on. The kind of gold the sky looks even bluer. Wind, but not too much, slight chill, but not too much. Then gray squirrels dash out from the cover of the woods, scramble around, and dash back. One, then another, then three or four more, scamper into the yard, pause a millisecond, race back. I kneel in the garden, knees pressed to dirt, pick hornworms off pepper plants. I know I will blow my cover, but I walk to the backyard to investigate. On the lawn, about a half a dozen ripe pawpaws, green skin tinged with gold, sweet scent of ambrosia. On the upper branches of a slender, leggy, pawpaw tree the golding leaves rattle. More squirrels, about four of them, chatter down at me, scolding. They want me to walk away so the harvest can resume.

Fruit too high for me
flung down to the leaf-strewn ground
gold in all pockets.

Contributors

Katarena Altier: I am a digital illustrator based in Athens, Ohio. My art style involves breaking down the world into color and shape to create a stained glass effect. I have been featured in TWANG Anthology in 2020 and a Las Laguna Art Gallery online exhibition in 2021.

Emily Anderson first learned about the pawpaw in 2018—starting a thesis on updating the nutrition information of the pawpaw at Ohio University. Emily loves talking about the pawpaw and attending the Ohio festival with her family. When not talking about the pawpaw, Emily is with her cats, Kiwi and Mango.

Chelsie Azbell is from southeastern Ohio. She enjoys painting and drawing. Acrylic is her preferred medium. She has one child and one cat.

Jason Baldinger is a writer and photographer from Pittsburgh. His newest books include *American Aorta*, and his first photography collection *Lazarus*. You can hear him read from various books on band camp.

Tom Barlow is an Ohio writer of poetry, short stories and novels. His work has appeared in journals including *Ekphrastic Review, Voicemail Poetry, The North Dakota Quarterly, The New York Quarterly, The Modern Poetry Quarterly*, and many more. See more at tombarlowauthor.com.

Alyssa R. Bernstein teaches philosophy at Ohio University. She has lived here in Athens for over two decades and has been happily married to a native, Todd Bastin, for nearly that long. Alyssa is extremely lucky to have landed here! They luckily have a wild pawpaw tree in their back yard.

Rob Brannan is a food scientist who has been studying the pawpaw for many years. He is intrigued by the many shapes, colors, sizes, and textures of the fruit. Rob recently began to paint pawpaws in oil, although he only has the courage to paint whole, intact pawpaws

Jennifer Browne is a curious critter trying to be in love with the world. She has some poems in chapbooks—*Whisper Song* (tiny wren publishing, 2023) and *The Salt of the Geologic World* (Bottlecap Features, 2023)—and journals, including *Steel Jackdaw*, *Gargoyle*, and *Humana Obscura*. She lives in Frostburg, MD.

Natalie Burton is a poet, teacher, and storyteller. She is currently working on a fantasy series and plans to attend graduate school for a master's degree in creative writing. Natalie lives in rural Ohio with her family and cats. She loves the outdoors, history, and traveling.

Stephanie Campsey was raised in Columbus, Ohio, where her first pawpaw was discovered on OSU's campus in 2001. Stephanie has lived in Athens, Ohio, for the majority of the past twenty years and has been an avid fan of foraging for native foods and attending the pawpaw festival. Stephanie has three wonderful boys who have grown up enjoying the wonders of wild edibles.

Grant Clauser lives in Pennsylvania. His sixth book, *Temporary Shelters*, is forthcoming from Cornerstone Press. His poems have appeared in *The American Poetry Review, Greensboro Review, Kenyon Review* and other journals. He's an editor for a news media company and teaches poetry at Rosemont College.

Rebekah Cotton grew up in rural central Ohio, where she developed a taste for pawpaws and writing. These days Rebekah lives in northeast Ohio with her husband, dog, and cat and enjoys taking classes at Literary Cleveland.

Lucia Carver Daniels: I'm in 4th grade at the best school in the world. I'm the label designer for Happy Hollow Brewing, and I love the Pawpaw Fest!

Maeve Denshaw: I am from Pittsburgh, Pennsylvania. I have a lifelong love for poetry and its ability to draw out the deepest and most important emotions in people, and I am so honored to be a part of this project. I grew up exploring the local wilderness around my house, and the pawpaw was one of the things what drew me to learning more about the land that I live on. It also taught me the importance of patience, dependability and the relationship which we choose to have with nature.

Cody Dikis: I really like anything to do with art. I enjoy so many mediums of art, including both traditionally and digitally, along with sewing for fursuits. I enjoy being involved with the local community and have always had a blast at the Pawpaw fest!

Ross DiPenti is an artist living and working on a 10 acre forest farm in Meigs County, Ohio, where he spends time gardening and managing his property.

Chris Farrell: Died to my 'SELF' and was spiritually regenerated by God-"born again," if you please, to be a New Creature in the Body of the Christ Jesus: Forgiven of my sin and given the Gift of life eternal! Thanks be to God!"

Sherry Deskins Goodson has been married to Brett for 48 years. She has two sons: Ross and Hunter. She also has two grandsons: Reece and Rylan. Sherry has been painting in watercolor since she was ten years old. It continues to be a wonderful journey. This pawpaw bloom image was taken from a photo by a local Palm Beach Post photographer.

Ikaika "Kat" Grimm really likes art. I mostly draw with paper & pen but I like doing watercolor too. I like cats, and cats are what I mostly paint. Cats are what inspire me. My nickname is also Kat. I also have four pawpaw trees in my backyard, they are blooming now!

Kari Gunter-Seymour is the Ohio Poet Laureate. Her collection *Alone in the House of My Heart* received the "2023 Best Book Award" from American Book Fest. She is the founder/executive director of the Women of Appalachia Project and editor of its anthology series *Women Speak*. Her work has been featured on *World Literature Today*, *The New York Times* and *Poem-a-Day*.

Jessica Held is an artist, teaching artist, small business owner, festival coordinator, and art editor living in Athens, Ohio. She enjoys family time, travel, painting, photography, teaching art, and coordinating the beloved annual Ohio Pawpaw Festival. Follow Jessica @fluxandfunction and @jessica.teaches.art

Orinn Hohenstein (He/Him) is a lover of nature, art, and music. He nerds out about lots of topics. He is a collector of things and tries his hand at many different hobbies. Orinn believes it's great to be weird. ❤

Byron Hoot was born and raised in West Virginia. Gone for five years only to come back to Appalachia to marry, have kids and work. Now retired in The WILDS of Pennsylvania. Read and write. Hunt and fish. Read an occasional poem or two. Life's been good.

Haven Horton-Kunce is an environmental studies scholar that fell in love with Southeast Ohio, Appalachia, and pawpaws through their time spent in Athens, Ohio, for their undergraduate degree.

Attila Horvath: Ironically, eating a pawpaw makes me break out in hives. Life can be cruel.

Jay Hostetler is a woodworker who makes "trees from trees." He gives different species of trees new life as works of art. Jay's Trees can be carved, painted, dyed or have the bark still intact like these Pawpaw trees. Jay loves the unique green color of pawpaw wood.

Meredith S. Jensen is a writer, artist, and performer living in Athens County, Ohio. For employment, she develops museum exhibits; for enjoyment, she birds, hikes, gardens, reads, practices henna art, and makes lists. She resides in a hollow with her partner, orange cat, umbrella cockatoo, and occasionally two collegiate gremlins.

Heidi Joffe's poetry works into her obsessions, particularly with nature, environment, and place. Her peripatetic childhood has left Heidi with an endless search for home. "I have worked as a teacher, art therapist and yoga instructor, but my most important work was as a single mother, raising two wonderful children."

Sydney Joslin-Knapp is a multidisciplinary artist from Dayton, Ohio. From hand-embroidered patches to paper-based installations, she uses a wide range of sizes and materials, finding inspiration in her community and the things that fulfill her. Additionally, Sydney apprentices as a cake designer, expanding the ways she shares joy with others.

Jennifer Schomburg Kanke lived in Athens County off and on for about seventeen years, but now lives in Florida. Her poetry collection, *The Swellest Wife Anyone Ever Had,* about her granny's life in Appalachian, Ohio, is available this fall. You can find Jennifer online hosting the Meter Cute Interview podcast on Meter&Mayhem.

Diane Kendig's latest books are *Woman with a Fan* and the tribute anthology, *In the Company of Russell Atkins.* After 40 years away from Canton, Ohio, she moved back to live in the home her dad built after WWII, and she's planted two pawpaw trees there. Her website is dianekendig.com.

Jeri Kendrick is enjoying her retirement as an avid beekeeper, loving wife, mother and "Nana" to six grandchildren. She lives in Hamden, Ohio.

Jennifer L'Heureux: I believe everyone is an Artist and I see the proof daily in Athens County. I am honored to say I vended at the very first Pawpaw Fest and have since been a volunteer, sponsor, camper, and groupie. How special that every year this native fruit brings people from all over together to enjoy, create, and celebrate!

Jennifer Michelle Mayer is a mother, poet, editor, and MFA student at Ashland University. A native Ohioan, her love of nature features in her work with themes of family, home, community, grief, beauty, and healing.

Chelsea McClellan is a poet living in Northwest Ohio on their family's little homestead. You will find Chelsea in their home orchard tending to the young plants, including the pawpaw patch, or sitting in its midst tending to a life-long love of word and sound—of thoughtful discussions, music, poetry.

Wendy McVicker has found fertile ground in Athens, Ohio, for her secret inner poet to flourish. Athens has helped her cultivate the joys of creative collaboration and friendship, and share her love of poetry in multiple ways, including as poet laureate from February 2020 to the end of 2022.

Martha Gallagher Michael is a professor emerita of Capital University and has published poetry with *Pudding Magazine: Journal of Applied Poetry, Northern Appalachia Review* and Steinbacknow.com with artwork for both *Pudding Magazine* and Steinbacknow.com. She lives in Columbus with 2 dogs, Alfie and Ruthie, and Slim Shady the cat.

Jean Mikhail first came to Athens, Ohio, to study Creative Writing over thirty years ago and never left. She's published in *Sheila-Na-Gig online, The Northern Appalachian Review, Pudding Magazine,* and other journals and anthologies. Jean writes now more than she ever has.

Andy Milliken is a poor mud farmer living in a shack on the banks of the mighty Racoon Creek (the longest "crick" in the world) with his dog, Oscar, his guitar, and the banjalo his grandpa gave him.

Barbara Marie Minney is a seventh generation Appalachian, an award-winning poet, teaching artist, and quiet activist. She is the author of *If There's No Heaven*, the *Poetic Memoir Chapbook Challenge, Dance Naked With God*, and *A Woman in Progress*. She lives in Tallmadge, Ohio, with her wife of 42 years. Follow Barbara at www.barbaramarieminneypoetry.com.

Tina Moore is the poet-in-residence at Passion Works Studio in Athens, Ohio. She loves poetry, her family and sharing her words with others.

L.D. Nehls is a muralist, illustrator, and art educator living in Cincinnati, Ohio. L.D.'s work can be found at ldnehls.com or @LDNehlsArt on Instagram.

Paul M. Noser studied liberal arts for eight years. He has been happily married for fifty years. Nature of all kinds have always been a focus of Paul's life. Thus, this poem came naturally.

Matt Peters had his first pawpaw from a tree that Chris Chmiel probably planted. He is a member of the Heartwood coordinating committee, "People helping people protect the places they love," helping protect pawpaw habitat wherever they may grow.

David B. Prather is surprised to now have published three poetry collections, in which most of the poems utilize some part of the natural world: birds, bugs, trees, flowers, weeds. He was raised in wild West Virginia, but he makes his home in suburbia. Feel free to check him out at www.davidbprather.com.

Bonnie Proudfoot lives in Athens, Ohio. Her poetry, fiction, essays, and reviews have appeared in journals and anthologies. Her novel, *Goshen Road* (Swallow Press) was long-listed for the 2021 PEN/ Hemingway and awarded the WCONA Book of the Year. Her book of poems, *Household Gods*, was published by Sheila-Na-Gig Editions.

Amy Le Ann Richardson earned her MFA from Spalding University ('09) and is a farmer, writer, artist, and teacher. She is the author of *Who You Grow Into*, Finishing Line Press 2024, and her work is featured in multiple journals. She lives and works on her Kentucky farm.

Anna Robinson is an engineer by profession and artist by inclination. She finds intrigue in the Pawpaw fruit thanks to an introduction by her friend, Greg. Anna is encapsulated by nature and has been inspired to capture the intricacies and nuances of the pawpaw fruit.

Shei Sanchez's work can be found in journals and anthologies, including *Hawaii Pacific Review*, Women of Appalachia Project's *Women Speak, Still: The Journal*, and *Last Leaves Magazine*. A Best of the Net nominee, Shei can be found herding goats and writing in the woods at her farm in Appalachian Ohio.

Jennifer Schwirian: I'm delighted to be part of this anthology! Although I'm not a native of SE Ohio, I call Athens home. I graduated from OU, met my husband, raised my children and built a life here. There's just so much to love about this region— including the pawpaw!

Brenda Jean Searcy first heard the word "pawpaw," preceded by "way down yonder in the" and sung by her mother. Brenda planted a patch of her own so she could taste one 30 years later. A musician and gardener, she is now also an attorney in Athens, Ohio.

Larry D. Thacker's poetry and fiction can be found in over 200 journals and anthologies. His books include four full poetry collections, two chapbooks, as well as the folk history, *Mountain Mysteries: The Mystic Traditions of Appalachia*. His two collections of short fiction include *Working it Off in Labor County* and *Labor Days, Labor Nights*, as well as a co-authored short story collection, *Everyday, Monsters*. His MFA in poetry and fiction is from West Virginia Wesleyan College. Visit his website at: www.larrydthacker.com

Patricia Thrushart writes poetry and historical nonfiction. Her fifth and latest book of poems, *Goddesses I Have Known*, was put out by Quimbey Pickford and Cheshire Publishing and benefits Clarion SAFE, a domestic violence shelter. Her poems have been published in numerous journals.

Andrew Alexis Varvel is a writer, researcher, and artist who lives in Bismarck, North Dakota.

Jessica Weyer-Bentley has two collections of poetry published; *Crimson Sunshine* and *Down Below Where the Canary Sings*. She has work published in countless anthologies and magazines. Jessica grew up in the hills of Eastern Kentucky and resides in Northwest Ohio. She is a proud Wife and Mother.

Kristine Williams lives and writes in Athens, Ohio, and is retired from teaching, in-person and online, public speaking, interpersonal communication, and writing courses at Ohio University and a local community college. Her chapbook, *Like an Empty House* (Finishing Line Press), came out in 2021.

Renee Williams is a retired English instructor from Nelsonville, Ohio. Her poetry has appeared in *Of Rust and Glass, Verse-Virtual, Deep South Magazine, Panoply, Impspired, Sein und Werden, The Rye Whiskey Review, The Amethyst Review, The New Verse News, and Beatnik Cowboy* among others. Renee takes orders from her cranky cat.

Katherine Ziff has lived in Athens with her husband Matt for twenty-six years and is retired from mental health practice and teaching. Some know her as the author of *Asylum on the Hill: History of a Healing Landscape,* a book about the early years of the Athens State Hospital. She tends a Pawpaw patch in their yard here in Athens.

Stephanie Kendrick is the 2023-2025 Athens, Ohio, Poet Laureate. She wrote *In Any of These Towns* (Sheila-Na-Gig editions, 2022) and is the editor of the local poetry newsletter, Periodical Poetry. With a Masters in Social Sciences from Ohio University, she serves her local community in a variety of ways, including through her career at the Athens County Board of Developmental Disabilities. She has been published in several amazing journals including *Gyroscope Review, Still: The Journal, Poets Reading the News, Pudding Magazine, Lunch Bucket Brigade, Sheila-Na-Gig online*, and elsewhere. Stephanie hosts Words and Wine on Wednesdays, a monthly open mic featuring poets and musicians from Athens County and beyond.

Stephanie's love for pawpaws began in 2018 when she started working for the Ohio Pawpaw Festival. Six years later, she is still working as a seasonal festival coordinator from March through September. It was through this work that she learned first-hand how the appreciation of a single fruit can lead to the creation of a community. Thousands of folks come together each year to celebrate the pawpaw. They share food, music, laughs, knowledge and stories. She hopes to capture an ounce of that magic in the pages of this book.

Sheila-Na-Gig Editions

www.ingramcontent.com/pod-product-compliance
Lightning Source LLC
Chambersburg PA
CBHW051636120626
46551CB00014B/2112